Generations' Inspirations

Poems to
Read Aloud

by

Anna B. Adair

and

Kevin Adair

Plus a Bonus Preview of:
I Wonder Why the Butterfly.

Generations' Inspirations   Poems to Read Aloud

Cover illustration by Jamie Reda

Cover design by Kevin Adair

The drawings accompanying poems by Anna B. Adair in this book were originally in publications produced by the Homewood, IL Women's Club.

I Wonder Why the Butterfly illustrations by Bill Wilkison

Butterfly illustration on p.106 by Rose Marie Winebrenner

ISBN: 0-9716251-1-5

Published by Do Things Records & Publishing, Inc.

www.DoThings.com

P.O. Box 6101 Chicago, IL 60680

Copies of *Generations' Inspirations: Poems to Read Aloud* are available at special discounts for bulk purchases by corporations, institutions and other organizations.

To Generations

Past, Present and Future

VISION EXCITES.

Love Unites.

And To Caryl, Warren, Bob & All of Our Family

Generations' Inspirations   Poems to Read Aloud

Table of Contents

Poems by Anna B. Adair (ABA)

Poems by Kevin Adair (KA)

Big Book Bonus!

Pages 88 – 106

Feature a Sneak Preview of the

Upcoming Illustrated Poem Book:

I Wonder Why the Butterfly.

by Kevin Adair

Illustrated by Bill Wilkison and

an illustration by Rose Marie Winebrenner

Preface

Boxes and boxes of poems, papers and plays—the legacy of a lifetime of writing left behind by my grandmother—sat untouched for over 20 years in my parents' basement. No fires or floods destroyed them, so there they waited patiently for someone to give them some deserved attention. There they might still sit, but that my parents emptied the homestead for their retirement accommodations. What better impetus to dig through those discolored boxes and give their contents new light? As the boxes sat untouched, I've filled a bit of my pauses between shows jotting down thoughts that from time to time have come in rhyme. As I looked through her papers, I was inspired to write the first poem in this book…the first two words of the title. It's a short poem, but I think it says a lot. Who would we be if not for the inspirations of generations past? Do we receive not only the oral history of our fore parents, but also a bit of their internal talents? I'd have to think so. Why should physical appearances be the only genetic inheritance from our kin? The creative of our species have often spawned creatives as well. This fact is often too much pressure on children of artists. It never was so in my family. Artistic achievements were always applauded, and artistic encouragements trickled down in subtle ways. I was always encouraged to get a real job; though I never did. Instead, I paid great attention to the family gatherings with chats such as, "Peter, how's your symphony coming?" "It's coming along well, Uncle Don. How's your latest book?" It's an interesting world when the average person's actions are seen as excellent in the outside world. It can be overwhelming, or it can spur one into action. When an active path is chosen, there's no time like the present! Inspiration comes in many forms. One of my other favorite short poems is

Poetry
Germinates.

My grandmother's poetry inspired me. Now hopefully her words and mine will spark growth in you. Many of my grandmother's poems were shared in hand-bound books produced by the Homewood Women's Club of Homewood, IL. Practically all of her poems won one women's club award or another. Some of her poems were also printed in newspapers and/or read on the radio. Over a half-century later, I've had the joy of sharing my poetry over the same WGN 720AM station where my grandmother's works were heard. My parents came down to hear the broadcast from the same Tribune building—where my mother worked many years before I was born. Strange how life has a way of coming back around again. The wisdom of old never goes out of fashion, it just finds new means of expression. In one of the Women's Club books entitled *Verses for Children* was the following foreword. Decades later, I share the spirit of their words. I hope you enjoy our journey through time as my grandmother's words and my own enliven a page or two for you!

Foreword:
It is hoped that the children might see a reflection of their own wonder-world in these verses, and that parents and teachers might find suggestions in them for other stories arising out of the everyday experiences of boys and girls.

—The Authors.

I hope that one of the ways readers are inspired by these poems is to create art. As you can see, in this book, most of the poems don't have illustrations, *yet*. If any poem gets your juices flowing, just take out a separate sheet of paper and draw a picture that you think would go with the poem. If you send your picture to me, I'll consider it for inclusion in future editions of this book. I can't send pictures back, so if you'd rather send a scanned high-quality color copy on a disk, that's fine too. Just remember to say which poem your picture is for, and send it to P.O. Box 6101 Chicago, IL 60680.

Poems to read aloud…
Which would make a Grandma proud.

I remember sharing early mornings with Grandma. She would call up the stairs when I visited her house. "Kevin!" she would call, loud enough to wake me but not to disturb my parents. Then I would join her as she made breakfast for the family. Pancakes and French toast were often on the menu, and we would have homemade jelly and apple sauce on them at least as often as we had syrup.

She was a formal lady. Her entire side of the family was formal and neat and punctual. But she smiled so dearly at her grandchildren with a sparkle in her eye that left no question of her warm heart inside. I never called her 'Grandmother.' It was 'Grandma,' or 'Gramma,' or even 'Gram.' I remember writing "To Gram" on one of my cards to her and being asked why I spelled it that way. I said, "Because she's not my 'Grand-Ma,' she's my Gramma. She's my Gram!" Because of her formal style, I'll generally spell my name for her as "Grandma," just as long as you know I'm hearing "Gramma" in my head. You know, I hope somehow and somewhere she's proud, even today!

10

As I began this journey, the act of digging through Grandma's writing inspired me to create on that moment as she might have created. The legacy we each leave behind gives those who follow a window into the life that was.

Passport Full of Memories

Page after precious page
Held so dearly year to year
Untouched now for decades
Yet their message remains clear
Poems sharing blessed dreams,
Which still ring true today
Awards and clippings turning brown
Which still all seem to say…
In each dear heart there dwells a poet
And a tender artist who
With support and care and nurture
Can share insights bold and true.
All art encouraged and set free,
To grow and share and see
Means aged artists never die.
Immortality.

Through her writing, Grandma has immortality. I hear her and feel her
in every word. In her writing, though, she confronts much mortality.
She wrote many poems about war and peace. My Uncle Bob went off
to World War II soon after high school. Grandma's grapples with life,
death and the great unknowns of war paint a progressive picture.

My Son –A Graduate

On the threshold of life I behold my son,
And I heard them say, "Well done. Well done!"
Though he won an honor and gained some fame,
To me a small boy he will always remain.

As I look at him now and the years ahead,
Wondering when and how and where he'd be led,
I know when he answers his country's call
He will do his best, he will give his all.

With countless others I see him go
To answer the challenge to meet the foe.
Gallantly, bravely, they'll turn the tide
And swing the victory to our side.

God! Speed the day, guide them safely through,
When life for them may begin anew,
That I might again behold my son
And hear them say, "Well done. Well done!"

Kentucky Skies
(To a Soldier in a Tank Battalion)

In most homes attention was focused on the ones who were gone and many letters and packages followed the boys to their training camps or to their fields of combat. The thoughts of one mother in Homewood, whose son was in training with an army tank battalion in Kentucky, were expressed in these lines:

Kentucky skies, be bright today
    And let the sun shine down
Upon a camp, among your hills,
    A teeming army town:
And somewhere there along the slopes
    You'll see a tousled Yank;
It won't be hard to find him
    For he's polishing his tank.

Kentucky skies, be clear tonight
    And let the moonbeams fall
Upon the silent barracks,-
    Until the Reveille call.
Before the coming combat, may
    He have sometime to smile;
So let your stars shine softly
    And let him dream a while.

--Published in "Wake of the News"
Chicago Tribune February 2, 1945

Bob and Anna B. Adair

A Letter from Overseas

All's quiet now, so I'll drop you a line
To tell you that I am feeling fine.
The sun is down, the lights are low,
I'm reveling in the candle glow.
I'm reminiscing a lot tonight,
So many memories pour in as I write.
'Tis for you and home that I deeply yearn;
May you be unchanged when I return!
May the old Main Street and the Pharmacy
Be just the same as they used to be!
There isn't much news, as we onward plod,
But I have kept my trust in God.
Though skirmishes may soon increase
In my own heart, I am at peace!

Anna, Caryl Mae, S.E. & Bob Adair

Comprehension

News of the war,
Bombings galore,
Skirmishes without end,
Fire and flack,
Troops driven back,
I simply can't comprehend.

But, the gleam in his eye
As he said, "goodbye,"
The wistful wave of the hand.
Things so worthwhile,
His radiant smile,
Yes, these I understand.

War affects all members of society from the oldest to the youngest. Grandma captured the spirit of many of the families whose children were at risk during World War II. How many of her sentiments still ring true today!

A Child's Prayer for Peace

God, be always very near
To the ones we hold so dear!

Bless the leaders of our nation,
Guide them in their lofty station,

Make them wise and just, until
They may always do Thy will.

Help those on a foreign shore,
So that war shall reign no more,

And each nation, like a brother,
Will try its best to help the other.

Bells of peace we then shall hear
God, be always very near!

Waiting for Peace

How eagerly the world is waiting
      For that day of peace
When an armistice is final, and
      The shock of war will cease.
When the tired, tortured earth is
      Freed from devastating might,
And all the martial madness will
      Have vanished with the night!

When bombing planes are grounded
      And blackouts are no more,
When the chatter of machineguns,
      At last, will all be o'er.
When the shrill cry of the shrapnel
      Is silenced once again,
When out of all the chaos
      Hope returns to men.

Then, peace will come so silently
      And be of life a part,
When goodwill, love and kindness
      Are enshrined within the heart,
When brotherhood and justice
      Will evermore increase,
Yes, eagerly the world is waiting
      For that day—of peace!

All along this journey into the past, I have been struck by the several similar themes that Grandma and I both literally explored. The human quest for peace is just as universal as our diversions into war. For this next poem, imagine a jazz combo of piano, upright bass and drums. Imagine a grooving audience, snapping along to the beat. Imagine a poet approaching a microphone. Imagine these spoken words rising out of that atmosphere.

Crack Me Off a Piece of that Peace.

Crack me off a piece of that peace, baby.
Crack me off a piece of that peace.
Crack me off a piece of that peace, baby.
Crack me off a piece of that peace.

Crack me off a chunk
Why not let's make it a great big hunk,
Oh, crack me off a piece of that peace, baby.
Crack me off a piece of that peace.

Y'all can keep all your tired old war
With that worn out talk about just one more
Face full of words,
I believe you least
When I hear this path you preach
That this, this, this is the war to bring lasting
peace...

Hold no doubt
That dodge is done
That's what they said about WWI!
Crack me off a piece of that peace, baby.
Crack me off a piece of that peace.

Crack me off a piece of that peace, baby.
Crack me off a piece of that peace.
Crack me off a piece of that peace, baby.
Crack me off a piece of that peace.

Now don't just let us all sit and sigh
No more innocents on Earth must die
Reach in yourself and get me high
Off a big ol' slice o' that sweet peace pie!

Oh, crack me off a piece of that peace, baby.
Crack me off a piece of that peace.
Crack me off a piece of that peace, baby.
Crack me off a piece of that peace.

Grandma loved and yearned for peace and fairness for all the people of the world. What a time it was in the 1940s when people at home joined in the quest to defeat Hitler's Axis powers. Americans at home worked by conserving gas and all of America's resources. The United States was in actual danger of being conquered by the direct threat of other countries which attacked us and declared war against us. The only hope for the future of the ideals of freedom was for the United States and her Allies to prove victorious. Oh, how my peaceful Grandma loved our rights and freedoms!

The Bill of Rights

We have a glorious heritage;
We have a sacred right
Which shields us from oppression,
From tyranny and might.

It makes our liberties secure
In times of calm or stress;
It guarantees the freedom
Of religion and the press.

It says that men may gather
In assembly, if they please;
Men of all creeds and races
May have these liberties.

The right of trial by jury
Is given the accused;

The fundamental rights of all
Must never be misused.

And now, our glorious nation,
Defender of the right,
To shield this sacred document,
Has risen in its might.

That all our priceless freedoms
May forever be retained,
That our children's children's children
May keep what we have gained.

We're all thankful for the sacrifices so many men and women have
made throughout our history! Grandma and I shared our love of
family. And the next few poems are all about a family's love.

Kevin & Muffin and Caryl & Warren (Mom & Dad)

My mother is Grandma's oldest child. Mom's personality and social position since she was very young was to take it upon herself to take care of others. When others hurt, Mom can literally feel their pain. Mom's done a great job of taking care of me, so she more than deserves a poem of her own.

The Caregiver

The Caregiver waits until all have spoken.
The Caregiver waits until all have their say.
The Caregiver listens and waits for her moment
To wipe any sign of discord away.
One says, "Always this way."
Another, " No! That way!"
But it's for common ground
      That the caregiver hunts.
"We'll have time for this way
      The next time," she'll say.
"But this time we'll just do it that way, this once."

Throughout her lifetime she's offered her care,
For the old and the young,
      Without question, she's there.
For all that she does she is under appreciated.
Yet at the same time she is oh, so appreciated.

The Caregiver works to take care of the home
To make sure that it's running as smooth as it can.

She leaves her door open to loved ones who roam
Then greets them with tastes
    From her cared-over pan.

She helps each of her charges
    Reach their destination,
Despite her men's leanings toward procrastination.

She's seen so many that she has cared for go by.
Still she is there and still she cares.
But in missing them sometimes
    She can't help but cry.

Did she do all she could do
    While they were still here?
How could she ever know?
Well, of course, she can't know.
So, how could she ever just let it all go?

Her arms aren't long enough
    To hold her heart's love.
Her heart is so great, she's a gift from above.

She sits and plays games
    With her lifelong love mate.

And she smiles with her lower lip
    Covering her top one.
She may lose a few more than she wins,
    But then wait…
That's not a reason that she'd want to stop fun.

Of who wins in the game, she just doesn't care,
She knows they both win,
    Because they're both there,
Just like when they sit side-by-side
    In their loveseat.
It is their time together that is truly a fine treat.

She loves her dear man through the thick
    And the thin.
Well, sometimes you lose and sometimes you win,
But then again, honestly, how would you feel?
When the thick and the thin is
    Forty years of oatmeal.

Sharing many a jam and fine pickles too.
A long lush life can have its fill.
Like current, grape, kiwi,
    Blackberry, and cherry,
Plus sweet, bread & butter, and even some dill.

The Caregiver shops and shops at Christmas.
She buys all the gifts, in full boxes and bags
Then carefully wraps them and adds all the tags,
Both from and to, so each person's included,
And none of the family or friends is excluded.
She is so thorough, as Santa's best elf
That she almost forgot to find one for herself.

The elderly dog is her constant companion.
The Caregiver's followed from room into room.
For person or pup she provides food a plenty,
But Dad takes the dog to the vet or the groom.

She's always turned to by those all around her...
Even a bit too often, it's true.
For all those around her are lucky they found her,
For everyone knows
        She will always come through.

How often poets exalt those who have gone by,
And might overlook the ones steadfastly there.
And so it is crucial the Caregiver knows,
Beyond words we are grateful
        To have lived in her care!

My dad, "The Handyman" has a poem of his own on page 28, and Grandma also expressed her love through poetic writing. Her youngest child was named Doris Ann which was abbreviated to "Dorie Ann." Gram watched and pondered and this is what she said:

The Little Red Chair

The baby stands by the little red chair,
She puts it here and she puts it there;
Wherever mother happens to be,
That little red chair you'll surely see.

And baby climbs on the little red chair,
To look through the window to see
What is there;
And then she'll shout and laugh with glee,
If there is something for her to see.

And then again her chair is a car,
In which she travels from afar;
The world is brighter for baby, fair,
Because of her friend, the little red chair.

A family fits together like a puzzle, and as Grandma observed so does life. Fitting this book together has been like a jigsaw puzzle for me: finding which poem goes best where and moving them all around until they fit. Many of Grandma's poems lay untouched and unread for decades until I started digging, and many of mine lay on scraps of paper in various drawers in my house. How amazing it was to see all the different subjects that Grandma and I both explored in our journeys through life!

The Jigsaw

Life is a jigsaw puzzle,
It's broken into tiny bits,
We try to piece them together,
Each little part, till it fits.

Each little word and action,
Each little deed each day.
Must somehow be put together,
As we go along life's way.

Each unkind word that's spoken,
Each good deed left undone,
Will mar the dainty fabric
Of the pattern being spun.

So, may we guide our actions,
And brave the trails we face,
That each piece of the intricate pattern
May find its proper place.

The Caregiver found her lifetime partner and our family found a puzzle master in the form of my dad, the Handyman. One of my joys of childhood was seeing my dad and my grandmother sharing time together. No inconsiderate in-laws in our house; everyone was glad the others were there. My dad shared with Grandma the benefits of conquering life's puzzles, and that was a lesson he shared with me from early on.

The Handyman

The Handyman pauses and watches and waits
As his young son, a puzzle, investigates.
"This is the right piece I can tell from the picture,"
Says the boy as his small fingers fumble and fidget.
"But it just won't go in, as I push it and press it.
It just doesn't work. No! I just can't get it!"

But the Handyman doesn't reach for the piece.
Doing it *for* him won't help his son to learn.
Rather, his hand calms the boy's shaking shoulder
For he knows success lies within one simple turn.
He teaches, "Now, Kevin, don't call it quits,
Don't force it, but turn it until it fits."

The boy's frustrations calm,
          And then he shouts, "Yes!"
For his dad has just taught him the road to success.

The Handyman came from a rough childhood.
"Children must only be seen and not heard"
Was taught with such force,
    It could make a heart harden.
"You must blindly obey and fit in our mold."
"Just listen to us and soon you will see,
We know better than you do,
    Of whom you should be."

For so many years he felt misunderstood.
He tried to obey them and follow their word,
But he found more true lessons
    From tending his garden.
For it takes a brave man not to learn all he's told.
People and plant both grow better, you see,
When supported and nurtured to be all they can be.

The Handyman always leaves the door open.
At the workbench there are often
    New things to share
With wood, hammers and nails,
    Saws, drills, planes and screws,
Each project's created with all the best care.

The same story is true
    When we're out in the garden,
Or fishing, or reading, or playing, or walking,

Or out playing catch in the biggest back yard.
No idea's out of bounds, not when *we're* talking.

The Handyman ponders and pauses to pray
     For a world which is better than it is today.
Then he works hard to make
     The world change for the best,
To give life's opportunities out to the rest
Who if given a chance would make their own way
And share in the better life after today.

For that which is right he takes a clear stand
And to folks 'round the world,
     He'll reach out his hand.
The Handyman has always a song in his heart
By sharing with others, he expresses his art.

Still he's also quite active right in his own house.
He's the one who is turned to to get rid of a mouse,
And to keep the plants inside and outside
     All growing
Or to help clean the driveway
     Because it's been snowing.

He'll happily split up a fresh fire log,
And dutifully bathe ears and hair of the dog.

Rub a dub dub
The dog's in the tub
But not like it much does she.

The Handyman's quite a baker
With his brand new bread maker,
Scores of bread loaves bakes he.

The Handyman makes everything he bakes
        Satisfying and nutritious.
Then he will fulfill your wishes...
        'Cause he even does the dishes.

From coffee or milk he'll take a big sip
And enjoys the taste so that he sports a fine grin.
But it falls to his wife to point out the drip
That somehow finds its way down
        To hang from his chin.

He knows that his family's the joy of his life
As he shares love and support
        With his Caregiver wife.
Sometimes it's those
        Who find life's love the latest,
Learn it was worth waiting
        For a love that's the greatest.

From his son's first moment on the Earth
The Handyman built him a groundwork for life.
He taught him respect for each being's worth.
And he helped him to see joy above any strife.

He taught him great patience
     And helped him to think:
When life presents puzzles you must never quit.
In all the worlds options you'll float and not sink
Just turn all the pieces until they all fit.

Such words only touch on the honor that he
     Knows in his heart he's so blessed to be
The son of the Caregiver woman,
     And the son of the Handyman.

Here's Grandma and her youngest child, Dorie Ann.

Poetry is a wonderful celebration, but it can also help a writer work through their most difficult times. The child that Grandma loved watching with her "Little Red Chair" never had a chance to grow up. Doris Ann Adair died of Rheumatic Fever, just a year or two before the Penicillin that would have cured it was widely available in the U.S. My grandmother was devastated. The dedication of the Women's Club's *Verses for Children* reads "For Doris Ann and All Children."

Reconciled

My singing time is over;
There's not much I can say.
My singing time is over,
For our child has gone away.
The child we loved so dearly,
With her cunning winsome way,
Brought joy and untold happiness
To us from day to day.
We planned so for her future,
She was so fair and sweet,
We thought that child would always
Have the whole world at her feet.
Our hopes and dreams were but in vain,
Yet, to His will we nod;
She brought a bit of heaven to us
And has gone back – to God.

Thankfully I've never lost a child so I can scarcely imagine that level of pain. The closest I have come to it is reflected in the poem I wrote in the final moments of my dog's life. I remember asking for a dog from at least the time I was four years old. My parents said no until my 14th birthday. Round about then, Grandma had said, "Kevin should have a dog." At the local pound a little brown Cocker-Doxie caught my eye. She was so pleased just to have eye contact with me through the cage that I couldn't get her eyes out of my head. Muffin was my closest companion for the next 18 years…even to her last day.

Muffin when she was 8.

One More Walk

One more walk before we go…
How those little legs have gotten slow.
We'll sit and share some family time
Before our final ride, our last goodbye.

When you were young, we'd run for hours,
Roaming through meadows,
Climbing rock towers.

We've had many a walk around many a block!

You'd scamper away, just a few steps ahead
Then you'd stop and look back

To be sure I followed.
In latter years, I lead the way.
We barely inched along today.
After the walks, then you'd get a treat.
And for 18 warm years you slept at my feet.

When you were a pup, we'd play tug and fetch.
You'd leap for a stick and catch hold of the sky.
You always had the clearest bright eyes.
I thought that they would never die.

Now those eyes have grown so dim,
And your floppy ears don't work at all.
It seems our walk is at its end
There'll be no shared summers, not after this fall.

Your little body's lost control,
Decaying around your still strong soul.
But before we take this final ride,
Just one more walk to say good-bye.

Sniff and tarry as you like to do,
Take all the time, I'll wait for you.

We made it all this way, my pup,
But autumn's a time for closing up.

Though hard for me, it's for the best.
It's time for you to take your rest.

But first, there was time for one last walk,
We relished each step around the block.

Kevin & Muffin in her last year

Family members are not the only folks for whom a poem can be the
finest form of tribute. When Uncle Bob was off to WWII, Grandma
was kept up to date on the war by the writings of a homespun reporter,
Ernie Pyle, who toured with the soldiers and wrote about his journeys.
His columns ran in newspapers around the USA. Near the end of the
war, when Mr. Pile was killed in battle, Grandma responded with these
words in rhyme:

To Ernie Pyle
(Upon occasion of his death, April 8, 1945)

Historian of the serviceman
    And always his true friend,
You wrote about the fighting fronts...
    And now all this must end.
You told the story of the war
    As he would have it told,
You shared his humor, hopes and fears,
    The weariness and cold.
You understood the terror
    Which often gripped his heart,
You knew his inner yearnings,-
    Of his life you were a part.
Your words revealed his longing
    With a unique skillfulness,
Conveyed his tender feeling,
    Which he couldn't quite express.
Although your pen's immobile now,
    Your words will live again,
Enshrined, with cherished memories,
    Within the hearts of men!

I felt a similar sadness and was also inspired to wax poetic upon hearing the news that Shel Silverstein had died. Shel wrote amazing children's poetry in such books as *Where the Sidewalk Ends* and *A Light in the Attic*. His stories were also groundbreaking. When you finish this book, go out and read Shel's *The Missing Piece Meets the Big O*. That story is one of the most engaging, poignant and concise Fables ever written. Mr. Silverstein was also a musician and composer for children and adults. One of his most famous songs, *A Boy Named Sue,* was recorded by Johnny Cash. A person of such diverse creativity deserves an appropriate tribute, and I was pleased to read this poem on WGN 720AM radio on January 6 & February 2, 2002.

A Tribute to Shel Silverstein

The writer is gone.
He can't come to play.
The flowers must bloom on without him this May.

He's packed up his kite
And his shiny new bike,
And the song in his head
That he thought you might like.

So much in his head
Was left to be said.
In pictures, in poems,
In songs that are silly,
In music so you can dance willy-nilly,

In stories that are somehow both funny and true,
So you laugh and forget that you
     Learned something too.

His eyes kept on looking
Which set his thoughts cooking
On all of the wondrous things you can find
In the Children's Department of your adult mind.

Now, he leaves it to you
To finish the stew.
Do you think perhaps you
Can be silly too?
So what do you say...
Why not try it today!

He'd love to play too,
But he's gone away.

Shel Silverstein   (1931-1999)

I never met Shel Silverstein, although I would have loved to. I did, however, poetically recall meeting a dear friend named Rosie Marie. Rosie is a singer and songwriter who I met while she and I were both performing at Chicago's Navy Pier. The happy tale of our meeting is well worth repeating!

A Happy Ode
(The Ballad of Rosie Marie)

How they'd gather to see sweet Rosie Marie
The pride of the Pier was she!
Then they'd all stay to hear.
No song was more dear,
Than a song by my sweet Rose Marie.

One day did we meet on dear old Dock Street
Where the Navy once docked a small fleet.
When she touch my hand,
I barely could stand,
I nearly fell off my feet.

But would she notice the guy
Who stood ten foot high
And juggled some pins
    By the sea?
Or would I just sigh
As she walked on by,
My beautiful Rosie Marie?

What did I try
    To capture the eye
Of beautiful Rosie Marie?

40

A quick magic trick
Or a well-balanced stick
So she'd smile at a guy such as me.

Right from the start, I spoke from the heart
To beautiful Rosie Marie,
"Whatever the weather,
We're better together!
So share life's sweet garden with me!"

Well, that's where it started,
and I've never parted
From beautiful Rosie Marie
If you like our song,
Why not sing along,
In a world where sweet hearts can fly free!?

Rose Marie and Kevin

The act of writing can help a poet find closure for happy and sad moments in life as it did for Grandma and me. Closure itself is another theme we both explored.

Doors

There comes a time in each one's life,
    When it's time to close the door.
Upon some vexing incident………
    Which comes up o'er and o'er.

The door of disappointment
    Should not remain ajar;
If we could close it quickly,
    'Twould better be by far.

Little misunderstandings
    Would often be put aside,
If the door of love and sympathy
    Were opened wide.

When we've passed
    Through the door of sorrow
    It too must be closed, and then
To a happy, hopeful future
    It should be opened again.

Closing a door is much like…

Turning the Page

The time has come again, my friend
For this page to come to an end.
We must pause and ponder what we've learned…
Then give this mighty page a turn.

One of the best times in life to ponder the past is when we move
from one home to another.

Reflections on Moving Day

The big house is empty…we'll soon be away;
There's something of sadness on moving day.
So many memories this old home now holds;
So much of life, as it unfolds.

Laughter of children… laughter and tears,
So much of living, down through the years.
Even deep sorrow that came our way,
Deep and relentless—it had its day.
On this day of parting, what can we give?
For in our memory, this old home will live!

Slow Progression

Forward progress delayed by a stoplight and a train.
Traffic, asphalt,
Vans, pickups and SUVs passing me.
I in the left lane stopped, they inching along in the right,
Able to make the turn at the light,
Slowly passing my left lane siblings and me
Going nowhere until the train opens the road.
Is this a neighborhood?
It once was. Once, trees lined this road.
Before the ever widening highway
Claimed this route for commerce.
No parkway to cushion the pedestrians from the street.
Traffic pressed against the sidewalk.
Sidewalk swallowing up the yards.
My van is filled with my history.
Headed to storage. Parents' house is sold.
No room in mine for these objects of past memories.
Still, in going through them, only some can be let go.
Grad schools I'm not looking to attend.
Finally their brochures are discarded.
They beacon a younger me to them.
He resisted their call.
Perhaps he should have explored more of Europe.
Still, Chicago is a beautiful way to spend one's twenties.
That road led to my love
Who's so alive in my heart,
          And in my house, and in my head.

So who can argue?
So few can claim that and still be honest.
Moving on from the past.
Old rejection letters are recycled.
The college and high school class notes, the old papers
and poems, cards of congrats, all still deserve a place,
So they'll be stored for $70 a month
In the orange-doored rent-a-basement down the street
From my parents' new seniors' community.
They'll no longer be mowing or shoveling snow.
Their new challenge is condensing the backyard garden
Into the bounds of the tiny patio outside their door.
Leaving our house full of memories behind
For a new family's memories.
Rain on my windshield, wipers on delay,
Occasionally squeezing the window clear.
Weather not stopping the workman nearby
Strapped to a tree trunk, branches long gone.
Chainsaw severing a two-foot segment above his chest;
He pushes it away to fall and stops the chainsaw.
The saw drops to hang from his belt as he lowers himself
And his straps two feet further. Again secure,
He retrieves the saw, starts it and begins to truncate
The next segment, just above his straps.
Soon the tree will be down and he'll be on the ground.
But now the train allows our gradual flow to go forth
Past the vanishing trees and memories and beyond.

Sometimes the words spoken to a poet roll around in their head and come out in a poem from the perspective of another person. Grandma recrafted her son's words into a poem for **A Letter from Overseas** on page 12. Letting words reflect has a healing effect—to help you leave the drear and have some cheer.

Cheer up.

Cheer up, my darling, don't be sad.
Cheer up, my darling, things aren't so bad.
Cheer up, my darling, I'm still your girl,
And you'll always be king of my world.

Cheer up, my darling, don't be sad.
Cheer up, my darling, things aren't so bad.
Cheer up, my darling, bright days are ahead,
Let my love in your heart bring a smile instead.

Cheer up, my darling, it's best to let go.
What's past is past, and this I know,
First we mourn a mistake then we move on to live.
We may find ourselves the hardest ones to forgive.

Some of us are very much in need of self-forgiveness. And, we can all use improvement.

Who?

Who likes disappointment?
Who wants to be afraid?
Who works to lose a lover?
Who fails when they can help it?
Who seeks a dead end road?
Who yearns for less success?
Who begs the mediocre?
Who strives to fall again?
Who prays to miss the boat?
Who can't wait to drop the ball?
Who emulates the average?
Who hopes to love a loser?

And yet we do.   Pooh!

On the other hand, there are parts of life designed just to make others happy. There's nothing like the day when the circus comes to town. I don't specifically recall reading or hearing Grandma's poem about the circus when I was a child, but perhaps it contributed to my lifelong fascination with the circus arts.

The Circus

Hurrah! Today is circus day,
    It's coming to our town;
I like to see the elephants,
    The monkeys and the clown.

I like to see the animals
    Do all their cunning tricks,
As climbing over fences
    And jumping over sticks.

I like to see the acrobats
    Swing in the air so high;
Or ride upon their ponies
    As they go racing by.

I wonder how they ever learned
To do so many things,
As walking on a narrow rope,
And swinging on the rings.

I'd like to be a circus-man,
A funny clown I'd be;
And thus make others happy
As they have oft made me.

How wonderful it was to come upon her circus poem, as I have worked with several circuses over the years, and I make my living using stunts and stories to bring smiles to others. Writers and circus folk share in the joy of entertaining folks and sparking imaginations. Gram never saw my circus shows, but she came to many of my children's theatre shows. For years now, I have combined the joy of rhyme with my juggling skills. Thousands of kids have laughed along with Juggling Icicles.

Juggling Icicles

Juggling Icicles, Juggling Icicles
Juggling, juggling, juggling,
Juggling Icicles!

I like to juggle them high.
I like to juggle them low.
I like to juggle them practically
Everywhere I go.

I like to juggle them near.
I like to juggle them far.
I like it over here…
And I like it over thaar!
I like to make them spin…
Again and again and again.
I can juggle them where I stand
Or I can juggle them in Backwards Land.

I like to juggle them high,
Way up to the sky!
To see as high as I can throw,
Everyone say, "One, two, three, go!"

Juggling Icicles, Juggling Icicles
Juggling, juggling, juggling,
Juggling Icicles!

I like to juggle them meek,
I like to juggle them bold.
But I can't juggle them very long, 'cause
They're very, very, very, very, very, very…
Cold!

Kevin and his Icicles

Rosie Marie is still performing too. She sings and tells stories to kids at schools and libraries, and they just love her! One of her performances that I attended inspired me to write about a little boy in her crowd. His name is Tommy, and he had quite a day.

Tommy

Tommy had tears today.
Tommy had tears today.
Tommy had tears today.
But now it all seems to be o.k.

Y'see, Tommy was shy
And his shyness was why
When all the kids were asked to join the show
It was Tommy alone who shook his head no.

So all the kids came to the front of the stage
And they sang to the song,
And they danced right along
Except little Tom, who sat with his mom.

And soon it was clear
There was nothing to fear.
Then he started to hate
His decision to wait.
When he had said no,
He won't be in the show.

So he sighed out, "Oh, great,
Now I guess it's too late."
And because of his fears
His eyes filled with tears.
And because he was shy,
He started to cry,
When he heard the fun song
With kids singing along.

His mom somehow knew
Just what she should do.
She took his small hand
And he started to stand.
To the stage went young Tom!
(Along with his mom.)

And he sang with the song
And he danced right along.
And away went his frown
And his mom went and sat down.

Now Tom smiled to know
He was part of the show!
In spite of his fears,
And in spite of his tears.
That's why I can say
Things turned out o.k.

And although he was shy
And he started to cry,
Tom's terrible frown
Had been turned upside-down.

Tommy had tears today.
Tommy had tears today.
Tommy had tears today.
But still I can say…
Yea!!!!
Tommy had a great day!

Tommy lamented not going up on stage with the other kids, but his mom saved the day just in time. I find myself thinking a different kind of lament when I am trying frantically to leave the house and I would, except for one problem.

A Departing Lament

Of pockets I have many,
Of keys I have few.
Oh, what,
Oh, what,
With my keys
Did I do?

Sometimes we find what we're seeking. People have been seeking a rhyme for the color "purple" for hundreds of years. My fictional friend, Vin, thinks he's found one.

Vin's Purple Poem

I seeks to find a rhyme for purple.
I seeks and seeks it all the time.
And then my mind comes up with "yourpull"…
Which is different from the pull that's mine.

Sometimes people don't find what they seek; or sometimes even when they do, they still can't keep their connection for very long. Rosie Marie and I connected to create a song that she has recorded on one of her CD's. The words of that song make a fine poem on their own. Sometimes everything seems so right, but things still find a way of unraveling.

I Missed You by That Much.

Chances come up in life,
Gotta grab them at once.
Sometimes there ain't no twice.
Sometimes a window's open wide,
Plenty of time to jump inside.
Some things will always be,
Some things can never be,
And some come down to, "Well, we'll see."
So it was for you,
So it was for me.
I missed you by that much, baby.
Baby, by that much.

I liked you,
You like me.
Thought that it was meant to be.
Some fate rushed in, I don't know what.
Seems our window just slammed shut.

I barely kissed you,
Still, oh how I miss you.
So much, baby, far too much.
Till I'm old and gray,
I'll think back to that day.
I missed you by that much, baby.
Baby, by that much.

I see kids playin', riding bikes.
I wonder what would ours be like.
I missed you by that much, baby;
Missed you by that much, baby;
I missed you by that much, baby.
Baby, by that much.

Grandma and I shared in the fascination of young minds coming to grasp with the world's shared reality. It's often a child who can help us look anew at the world that we've gotten used to.

Rollerskating

Up and down the street we glide
    Rollerskating, side by side.
What fun 'twould be, if we twirled
    On rollerskates around the world!

Observation

A four-year old was playing
    And talking to her Dad;
She noticed he was tired
    And he looked a trifle sad.
Her childish voice resounded
    When everything was still,
"I think Daddy will be a Grampa
    Before my Mommy will!"

Grandma with her niece, Bonnie

Logic of a Three-Year Old

"Where are you going, Ennie Ann?"
"I want to go with you
I hope I can!"
"When you're a bit older," answered I,
"To the big stores I'll take you
By and by."
A period of silence…
Then she said with a bow,
"You know, Ennie Ann……
I'm a bit older now!"

More Children's Logic

Three years older than me?
Is that what you say?
Three years older than me?
Not after today!
I'll catch up someday,
Then you will soon see!
'Cause my birthday's in March
And yours isn't until May!

My Birthday

Tomorrow is my birthday,
Oh yes, I know the date;
I'm going to have a party,
And I can hardly wait.

My mother planned the party,
For all my friends and me;
She asked them to come early
And stay till after tea.

We're going to play so many games,
And have just lots of fun;
I know that everyone will say,
They're glad that they could come.

We'll have the finest things to eat,
Ice cream and lemonade,
And then there'll be the candles
On the cake that mother made.

Oh, I'm so very happy,
I don't know what to say;
I wish I had a birthday,
About every other day.

A Wish Fulfilled

Here's to wishing
I was fishing.
It's not the one that got away,
But all the fun we had that day.
I lost the fish but won't be sad,
I got to spend the day with Dad!

My mom often knits gifts that are warming. A scarf from her keeps
me warmer than a similar scarf from any other source.   How nice it
was to find a poem from Gram about knitting in 1948.

Knitting

Knitting, purling, bobbins shaking,
Argyle socks are in the making!
Is she dreaming of romancing,
Or perhaps of some one dancing
In the argyles she is making?
Kitting, purling, bobbins shaking!

Thanks to Grandma, when my mom was a kid (and then later when I was a kid) our family had a very special time. When company was coming the whole world stopped to focus on making everything the best for the company.   The arrival of company is a timeless connection in our house between children and parents. When I first read this poem to my mom she said oh, how it took her back!

Company's Coming!

Company's coming!
Don't make a mess.
Company's coming!
Time to get dressed.
Company's coming!
Wear your good shoes
Company's coming!
There's no time to lose.
Company's coming!
Go pick up your room.
Company's coming!
I'll get out the broom.

Company's coming!
We'll just shut *that* door.
Company's coming!
I just mopped the floor.
Company's coming!
It's as clean as you please.
Company's coming!
Got down on hands and on knees.
Company's coming!
So go wash your hands.
Company's coming!
Don't slouch when you stand.
Company's coming!
They've come from so far!
Company's coming!
Did I hear a car?
Company's coming!
Oh, yes. Here they are!

Grandma would watch as I explored her bookshelf. So many books by so many authors right in the living room where no T.V. was allowed. The living room was for company and for reading with no modern distractions. Reading is an insight into the past. A book is the oldest form of time travel. Others have made it through their problems, and we can make it through ours too. Now that same bookcase of Grandma's is in my living room, where TV is also not allowed.

Among the Books

Recently, I tried to ponder
What a friend a book can be,
What a true and wise companion,
What exotic company!

What a treasure when we're lonely,
What a help when we are sad,
What a comfort when we're troubled
What a joy when we are glad!

Oh, how much advice and council
Just a single book can give,
As in fancy, we can wander
Into other realms to live!

Children's developing minds are so tender and so dear that as adults we have to be careful what examples we give them to emulate. Do we provide good examples? How will people of the future look at the lessons we teach children today? Positively as in this next poem…

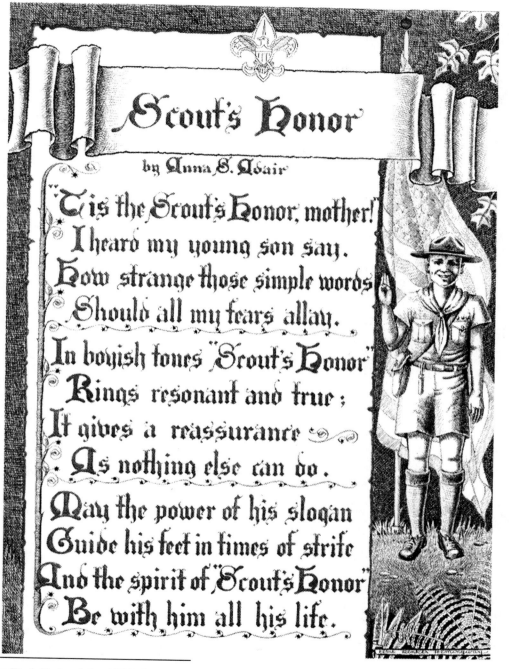

Scout's Honor

by Anna S. Adair

'Tis the Scout's Honor, mother!
    I heard my young son say.
How strange those simple words
    Should all my fears allay.

In boyish tones "Scout's Honor"
    Rings resonant and true;
It gives a reassurance
    As nothing else can do.

May the power of his slogan
Guide his feet in times of strife
And the spirit of "Scout's Honor"
    Be with him all his life.

Published in "Wake of the News" *Chicago Tribune* February 13, 1939 and in various Boy Scout magazines.

65

…Or perhaps not so positively?

Honorable?

Little boy! Little boy!
Please go away.
Little boy! Little boy!
You can't play here today.
Little boy! Little boy!
We don't want you around.
Little boy! Little boy!
Get out of our town.
Little boy! Little boy!
We don't care what you say.
Little boy! Little boy!
If you're gay you can't stay.

The honor of old was to grow and to share
To make bonds with others and find ways to care.
Through power and force
        They've stolen our history.
Why nobody stopped them is a sad sullen mystery.

The world's a diversified garden of arts
How sad when authorities harden their hearts!
Perhaps they yearn for lost affection
And take it out in your direction.

From fear that they might want to kiss you,
With hardened hearts they turn and dis you.
And yet the hallowed slogan still chimes…
"To help other people at all times?"

They used to slam other races, or women or Jews,
And the sad story is that sometimes they still do.
They say that your love is something you choose,
And they make that their reason
    That they attack you.

But the future is changing; there'll be a new day
When these hates of the past have all swept away.
When hunger and turmoil
    We've all worked to solve.
Once we've helped the closed minds
    And hearts to evolve!

So that some day they'll say,
"Little boy come and play.
Just be who you are.
Who you are is OK."
Little boy, little boy, don't run away.
Just be who you are, and please stay and play."

Times change. People grow—children and adults too. Grandma was born October 31, 1891; she lived into the 1980s. Thinking of all the advances she saw in her life boggles the mind. She was twelve when the Wright Brothers first flew at Kitty Hawk, NC and thus broadened the horizons of people everywhere. Initially, the term 'Aeroplane' competed with 'Airplane' for what the invention would be called. Call it what you will, expanded imaginations can never be made small again!

My Aeroplane

Wouldn't you like to go out for a ride,
    Up in my aeroplane?
Then we could travel for miles and miles,
    Faster than any train.

Over the tree-tops and over the hills,
    Over the cities too;
Over the mountains far away
    And over the sea so blue.

Oh, we could travel above the clouds,
    Farther than we can see,
Till we'd reach the other side of the world,
    And in foreign lands we'd be.

Ah! I only wish that my aeroplane
    Could do all those wonderful things;
For you see it really is only a toy,
    And I've broken one of its wings.

Seeking flight is a timeless human quest. For centuries children and adults have been finding ways for their spirits to fly!

Michael

Early in the morning
This laddie comes to play,
Early every morning
At the break of day.
He doesn't waste a moment,
Or sit around and brood.
Like wise men long before him,
He seeks out solitude.
And seeking, finds the morning
Fresh with morning dew,
And finds the sky at dawning
A muted shade of blue.
While all the other children
Were fast asleep in bed,
He got up this morning
And flew a kite instead.

Flight

He looks eleven; she's perhaps twelve.
Off to the park to Fly!
He holds the string stick and it lifts off.

Soar!

"Watch those wires!" she warns.

The sun paints streaks behind their heads.
Now the stick is hers.
"Let out more, let out more!"
They fumble together for control.
She has the stick, he grabs the string.

Loop, loop, loop,
spin, spin, spin, loop,
spin, loop, spin, dive,
spin, loop, spin,
loop, spin, spin, dive, CRASH.

He runs toward it.
She stays back, winding, winding, winding.
"Ready?! Ready?!"
He lets go and we soar again--
He, she and I –watching from my car,
Invisible to their world.

She smiles and hands it off to him.
His turn,
Her turn,
Four hands gently share the stick.

Gust! Loop! "P Spin! U Dive! L Loop! L

Cras...!"

…No! It's up again!!!!

String stretches across the park.
The baseball batting cage
        Reaches out a webbed metal hand.
Now the cage takes its turn and grabs the string.
The two stand in the mud of the baseball field.
Their eyes follow the flyer to the ground,
As their feet and hearts sink a bit.

The string remains trapped,
Looped over the cold
Metal cage.

She winds, winds, winds.
He runs to the cage and begins to climb.
Careful, careful, up…
About 12 feet straight up.
Then over the edge onto the slant.
Still about 8 feet to climb.
Climb and reach, climb—reach.

He pulls the string free from
The highest point—
The lip of the cage.
Carefully turns and smiles.

He sits, then begins to come down.
"Look!" he points.
A small plane glides overhead.
SLIDE. SLIDE!! Grab. Breathe!
Her eyes widen.
Pause, "I almost slipped!"

Down he climbs. Safe on the ground.
Something's wrong.

"Wasn't that piece here?"
"Can you fix it?"
"NO, that part's broken."
"Try it anyway; try to fly."

Up. Spin. Down.
Up. Spin. Down.
    Spin. Down.

"Will it go back?"
"No?"
He beats the injured flyer
With the piece that's broken off.

Their legs run again.
One more try?
She'll hold the stick this time.
Run! Run!

Off they run.
The string across her shoulder.
The flight continues
Inside them,
As the kite trails behind,
Scraping and bouncing,
Crumpled against the ground.

By the time the 1960s rolled around, the world's imagination and its
concept of flight had expanded to feature successful space travel, and
Grandma witnessed and celebrated every step of the way. Imagine
seeing news of the first plane flight as a child, living through both
World Wars, seeing television bring the world to your door and
following with excitement the first ventures into space! Imagine.

To the Apollo 11 Astronauts

For centuries man wondered and dreamed of a way
Of reaching and touching the moon some day.
With you and your spacecraft a-top Saturn Five
Man's hopes and dreams became alive.

For days and nights you roared through space,
An incredible pioneering race.
With technological problems to face
Before you could reach Tranquility Base.

You, who dared destiny, reached your goal;
From Columbia to Eagle, you had full control.
The lunar module made its descent;
"The Eagle has landed!"
          Was the message you sent.

When you made the first footprints
    On gray lunar sands,
When you gathered up rocks
    And moon soil in your hands,
We watched and listened in raptured delight
For we couldn't believe this breath-taking sight.

When you planted the flag in lunar dust
And stood at attention near the crater's crust,
The American banner stood proudly unfurled.
What a thrill for the anxiously waiting
        Earth-world!

From the lunar module, for the back-to-earth trip
Toward a rendezvous with the mother ship.
You witnessed the moon disappearing from view.
That bold dream of the ages had now come true!

I like to say, "Follow your dreams; no one else can!" And Grandma was all about following dreams. Many of our poems reflect the beam of a dream theme!

At First, 'Twas but a Dream.

Oh, every great achievement,
At first was just a dream;
A dream of great adventure
Or of conquest or a scheme,
Of doing things that never
Had been heard about before;
And then by planning, striving, doing,
Dreams were realized once more.

The tower or the monument
A gleaming in the sky,
Is the result of some great dream,
As slowly, by and by,
The work of art was finished,
Which at first was just a dream;
As evermore enhancing,
To the artist, it did seem.

The wonderful cathedral,
So beautiful and fine,
With its enchanted music,

Its melodies divine,
With all the lovely paintings,
So real they may seem,
Before they really came to be
They had been but a dream.

So, lets dream and labor onward,
Our work is not in vain.
We dream of things that could be done
Then we try again
To shape our deeds, to mold our lives
In such a way, that we
May someday see our dreams come true
And thus contented be.

--Broadcast WGN 720AM Radio,
December 5, 1948

Come Dream with Me.

Come dream with me a Digital Dream,
Where nothing is quite what it would seem.
Come walk with me to the digital station,
With the trains departing to the Imagine-Nation.

We'll leave all the Gotta-Doos
    And Musta-Bins behind,
While we hunt for all the Cuud-Bees
    That we can find.

Those Cuud-Bees are a dangerous lot.
They hide with the Sumdaes,
Near the town of Whyknott.

But if you are strong
And you'll come with me
With your eyes bright and open
And your heart light and free,
Then bravely we'll walk
Right through old Whyknott
And we'll visit such Sumdaes
That some have forgot.

Even past where most would see just a blur
Or get lost in the land of the fierce Neverwurr
We'll find all the best, the tremendous,
> The greatest,
The fastest, the oldest, the slickest, the latest,
Why, only the tip-top, the prime of the crop,
The most beautiful Cuud-Bee
That ever you would see.
It's a digital dream that once started, won't stop!

We will offer our best,
We'll be put to the test,
So never could we be
Left behind with the rest.

My most mighty methods must still be polite,
As I clearly use insight and kindly invite.
Then you and I will both do what's right,
With polite invite insight
> For each lovely Cuud-Bee
That we happen to see
To request that they journey with you and with me.
For there's no better partner
> Than a lovely Cuud-Bee.

Then they'll follow us back
    From the Imagine-Nation
And join-journey us home
    Through the Digital Station.
Then won't all dear friends clearly be so surprised
When we dance with the Cuud-Bee's
    They'd never surmised!

So dream with me now all the Digital Dreams
Where everything's more than just what it seems.
Hop mentally now from station to station
And visit your own private Imagine-Nation.
For all of the Digital Dreams you can see—
The Lightest, the Brightest,
The Latest, the Greatest,
The Top-ist, Won't Stop-ist
And even Elate-ist!
When you open your heart and let it fly free
And you open your home to just one Cuud-Bee!

The possibilities of chance bring various people together in each lifetime.
What we do with those meetings is up to us. Rose Marie and I connected and
created artistically. We have influenced, challenged, and inspired each other.
Rose Marie listened to some of my words; then she recrafted my concepts,
mixed them with her own and shared them back with me, to brighten my
journey. Thus came to be the next poem. She crafted my concepts with
thought and with care, revealing a vision of life you may share. Once you
find your dream, do you have enough steam to seek your goal and thrill your
soul?

Follow your Dreams.

I wanna look back on my life
And know that each choice
Has given me something to always rejoice.
I wanna live every moment I come to in full
And never be drowned by a negative pull.

The tides of chance ebb and flow,
The fruits of your garden bear what you sow.
The skies will be blue if you want them to be,
If you see what they show and
Know what you see.

Don't wanna be caught in the winds of despair,
I wanna be free, live my life like a dare.
Existence is fleeting, so I'll take a stand
To follow my dreams. No one else can.

Follow your dreams. Follow your dreams.
Seek out each mystery. Learn what it means.
Enjoy every journey. Play out every scheme.
Make your life matter, and
Follow your dreams.

But some dreams don't come true. Or some that do are too good to last. 'Happily ever after' is a fairy tale because each day of joy takes work to maintain it. Sometimes butterflies fly away. All we can do is let them go as we keep searching for brighter skies. The sadness we feel can make the good times feel all the more joyful. No one likes loss, but life wouldn't be life without it.

You Meant the World to Me.

Your touch haunts my hands
With faint phantom flesh.
The arms that used to hold you to me
Now fall aimlessly.
Your sweet lips have gone.
The taste lingers on…
With words that you once whispered to me,
"Oh my sweet tender dove,
You're my life and my love.
You mean the world to me!"

I stand by the sea.
The clouds hide the sun.
The wind which warmly carried my soul
Now blows right through me.
The waves call your name.
The birds fly away.
I wish that they could carry my dreams
To my sweet tender dove,
I'm your lost lonesome love.
You meant the world to me.

I cry to the fates
A song without end.
Alone in our love's promised duet,
My partner, my friend.
When life's love is lost…
One cannot count the cost.
Oh my sweet tender dove,
I'm your lonesome love.
You meant the world to me.

Much as we hate to let anything beautiful go, autumn must end to make way for winter, then spring. The changes of the seasons always captured Grandma's fancy.

Stay, Autumn, Stay!

Autumn breezes, softly blowing,
Red and yellow leaves are glowing.
Birds migrating, as if knowing
    That summer's nearly done.
"Now that the great out-doors is playing,"
That is what the old folks are saying.
Golden corn is lightly swaying,
    Swaying in the sun!

A fiery glow, the maple's turning,
Like the red oak, it is burning
With gay colors, as if yearning
    To be changed to gold.
Bushes, trees and plants are vying
With each other, somehow trying
To keep summer-time from dying.
    A picture to behold!

It would be a lengthy story,
To complete this category,

To fully tell of autumn's glory
    Before it slips away.
Life is ebbing, life is clinging,
Though the birds are southward winging,
Nature gently joins in singing,
    "Stay, Autumn, Stay!"

Wind of Spring

South wind!
Why are you blowing,
Blowing my hair about?
Blowing my big umbrella,
And turning it inside out.

South wind!
I know why you're blowing.
Blowing and calling so
You're calling the baby blossoms
Hiding under the snow.

The more some things change, the more others stay the same. One aspect of life that seems to never waiver is a grandparent's love! I felt Grandma's warm caring touch, her firm gentle hugs, and her focused direct guidance when I came upon this Grandma poem. Thinking back on those times, I'll always remember her sweet powdery Grandma aroma when she held me close and the delicious hearty smells of her stove that filled her house. I'll also never forget curling up with her to read to me. Her words are a lifeline to the past that we shared, as well as a welcome to future minds being formed. Let love and support be your guide in all times. Some ideals once voiced and shared can never die! Immortality.

Grandma Thinks

Who thinks a little boy
A great big bunch of joy
Why Grandma does, that's who.

Who thinks a little miss
Deserves a great big kiss?
Why Grandma does, that's who!

Who thinks a little lad
Is never, never bad?
Why Grandma does, that's who!

Who thinks a lassie wee
Is as sweet as she can be?
Why Grandma does, that's who!

Another stability in life is the benefit of reaching out to others for support and inspiration.

There You Are.

There you are, dear. You're my star, dear
Whither you're near or thither you're far,
Whither or thither, why, there you are!
If life deals a hollow or tough times to swallow,
Or the greatest dared dreams
     Really do come through,
It's not a no-brainer, nor a salt-water-sweater
But sooner and later, we're better together!

The next section of this book is a bonus, a preview, if you will. One of my most popular poems is entitled *I Wonder Why the Butterfly.* I am working with illustrator, Bill Wilkison, to create a full color picture book from this one poem. But rather than make you wait for that book to be ready, Bill has graciously agreed to let me include some of his drawings and sketches along with this poem so you could get a taste of what's to come. So now you can cast your eye on the *Butterfly*!

I Wonder Why the Butterfly.

Butterfly, Butterfly,
Why is it you flutter by?

Flutter by, flutter by,
On your way into the sky.

There's something I would like to know,
Just before it's, 'Off you go!'

In the air with just one leap,
What's this secret that you keep?

As you putter and you flutter,

Out beyond my bedroom shutter,

Just for me would you please mutter,

What have you to do with…

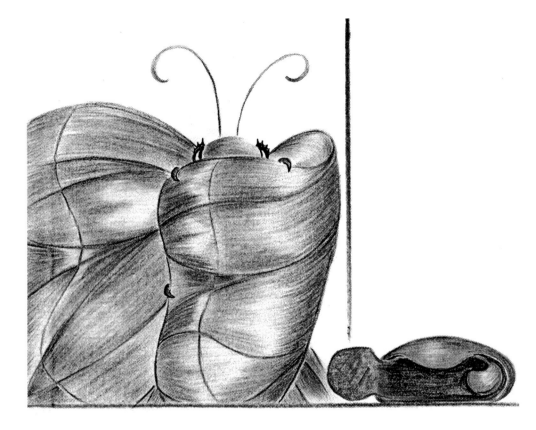

Butter?

Dragonfly, Dragonfly,

Now *you're* off into the sky!

As I stroll along the beach,
You stay just beyond my reach.

Perching on a boat that floats
Out upon the lake so blue,

I can't help but wonder why

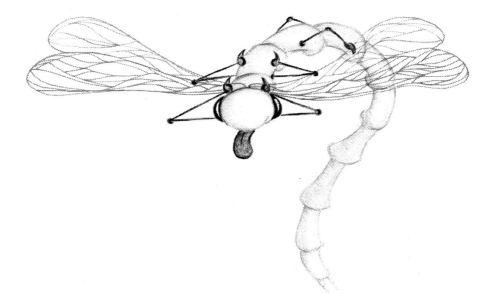

Your name is confusing too.

How your wings cut through the air!
So small and clear, they're barely there.

Landing lightly on my wagon,

You are the most dainty dragon.

Butterfly and Dragonfly,
Painting colors 'cross the sky.

Putting on a pretty show
High above their friends below.

Their shadows cause a moment's shade
On one who's leaping blade to blade.

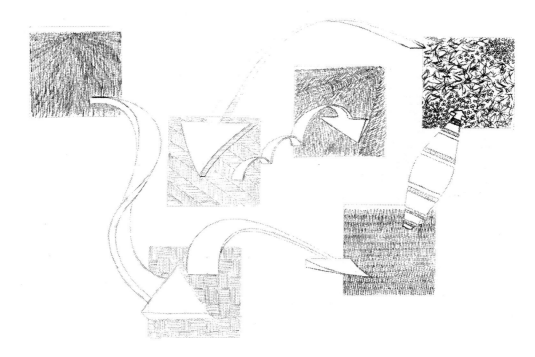

Gleefully and unafraid,
Bouncing all about the glade.

Can you guess who it would be...

Jumping, jumping, happily?

Here's a bug whose name's more proper.

B. Wilkison 2002

Indeed it is the green…

Grasshopper!

Here are some of the sketches that Bill used as he was developing the characters for *I Wonder Why the Butterfly*:

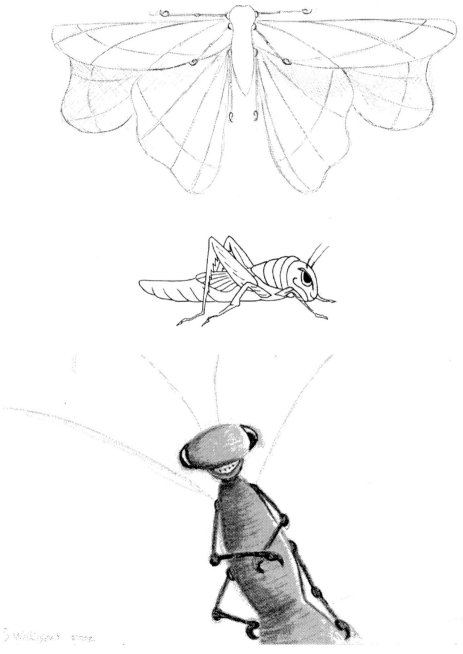

Before Bill and I started this illustration project, Rose Marie was inspired to create one picture for the poem. Here it is. One act of art can inspire so many others. Poetry (just like all of art) germinates.

Butterfly, Butterfly... Why is it you flutter by?

Bye-Bye,
Butterfly,
Bye-Bye.

The purpose of every book is to bring author and reader together. I feel closer with Grandma through this process of exploration. It's also been thrilling to work with all of the illustrators whose work these poems inspired. I hope you've found this book inspiring as well.

In Closing

If you liked this book, please let me know!
There's always further we can go.
If you'd like to have another look,
There's plenty more for another book.
We'll connect beyond all space and time
We'll share a bit of verse and rhyme.
Let's bring together our world's nations with:
Generations'   Inspirations'   Continuations.

Printed in the United States
70127LV00001B/52